WHO IS THE GREAT

Katherine Johnson?

America Selby

Ladies Image Publishing

Email: admin@myamazonauthor.com

Dear Reader,

If you enjoyed this book or found it useful, I would be very grateful if you would post a short review on Amazon. Your support really does make a difference and I read all the reviews personally so I can get your feedback and make this book even better.

If you would like to leave a review, all you need to do is click the review link on this book's Amazon page here.

If you are a member of kindleunlimited, I would be most grateful if you would scroll to the back of the book so I will be paid for your borrowed book.

Thanks again for your support.

America Selby

Table of Contents

Prologue

"I counted everything... anything that could be counted, I did."

Katherine Johnson has been called "the girl who loved to count". She has become famous as one of the subjects of a bestselling book by Margot Lee Shetterly, called Hidden Figures. The book told about black women math experts who helped put men on the moon. It was made into a movie, also called Hidden Figures, with Taraji P. Henson playing Johnson.

Before she became famous, she had to get an education and to work hard. She learned to make the most of the opportunities that came her way. Johnson, and most African-Americans, had to deal with prejudice. Prejudice is very unfair, this is when someone dislikes you just because you are different in some way.

Katherine Coleman was born in West Virginia in 1918. She loved to learn and ask questions, but she loved math most of all. A smart girl and good student, she was ready for high school at age 10. She graduated from high school when she was only 14. She went on to college right away and graduated from West Virginia State College at just 18 years old. Her special fields of study were French and math. A professor even created special math courses for her because she was so good.

After graduating, Johnson taught math and French at a high school for a while. Her college professors remembered how good a student she was and thought she should get more education. So, she was one of three black students picked to integrate West Virginia State's graduate programs. Graduate programs are for students wanting more education after college.   To integrate meant to have black and white students go to the same school. She dropped out after just one semester in the new program so she could start a family. She and her first husband, James Goble, had three daughters. When her daughters were older, she returned to teaching.

In 1952, she heard of jobs for math experts at the NACA, the National Advisory Committee for Aeronautics. The job was at a place called Langley in Virginia where aeronautical research was done. Aeronautics is the science of traveling through air and space. It would be good for the family since the salary was higher than Katherine's teaching pay. When James also got a job nearby, the family decided to move. Katherine started work in the summer of 1953 as a human computer. These were women who did math calculations for the research at Langley.

Her bosses soon saw that she was smart and was very good in math. She wanted to keep learning as well and asked many questions. She wanted to understand well the work going on at the center. Even though she smart and good at her job, she faced prejudice, such as some bathrooms being for white people only. She did not let herself become mad about these unfair things. She just decided not to let her race or gender keep her from succeeding and progressing in her work. Katherine faced troubles at home too. Her husband James died of a brain tumor in 1956, leaving her a single mother. She remarried in 1959, having met her second husband, military man James A. Johnson, at her church.

The NACA leaders kept giving her important work because they knew she would do her best.   When the Soviet Union sent the first satellite into orbit around the earth, United States officials got worried. They feared the country was losing "the Space Race" to the Russians. So they asked the people at Langley to do more research on sending objects and men into space. That is when NACA became NASA. NASA stands for National Aeronautics and Space

Administration. Johnson was part of the team that worked on the first two parts of the US space program. The Mercury Program put the first American in space. It also put the first American in orbit around the earth. The Apollo Program came next. It put American astronauts on the moon. Johnson and her math skills were important to both programs.

In 2015, she received the highest civilian award in the United States. The Presidential Medal of Freedom was presented to Johnson by President Barak Obama.

The Counting Begins

Katherine Coleman was born on August 26, 1918 in White Sulphur Springs, West Virginia. She was the youngest of four children born to Joshua and Joylette Coleman. The other children were Charles, Margaret, and Horace. Katherine's father worked at several jobs to support his family. These included being a farmer and a bellman at the Greenbrier Resort in the town. Her mother was a school teacher, a born teacher, Katherine would later say. Though her father had to stop going to school after sixth grade, both parents valued education. They wanted and encouraged all the children to go to college.

Katherine was especially eager to learn, even as a small child. She longed to go to school with her older brothers and sister. In fact, she sometimes followed one of her brothers to school and impressed his teacher with her abilities. She was reading at a young age, but especially liked math. She told people, "I counted everything. I counted the steps to the road, the steps up to church, the number of dishes and silverware I washed … anything that could be counted, I did." Her father was also good in math and Katherine felt she may have gotten her math talent from him. "He originally worked with lumber. He could look at a tree and tell how many boards he could get out of it," she told people later. The young girl was so smart and able that she was placed in the second grade when she got to enroll in school. She advanced through grades quickly and was prepared for high school at the age of ten.

Black and white students did not go to the same schools at that time. This is called segregation. White Sulphur Springs did not offer school for African Americans after the eighth grade. Some black students stopped going to school when they finished that grade. But Joshua Coleman wanted to make sure his daughter was able to meet her full potential. So he took his family to Institute, West Virginia. The Colemans enrolled Katherine in the high school on the campus of West Virginia State College. The college, since it started, had only taken black students. White students went to another college. Institute was 120 miles away from their home in White Sulphur Springs. Still Joshua felt it was important for her to continue her education. The family lived in Institute, with her mother becoming a domestic. A domestic is a person who helps take care of someone's house, like cooking and cleaning. Joylette took care of the children while Joshua returned home to work on the farm. When income from the farm was poor, Joshua moved into White Sulfur Springs and took the bellman job at the Greenbrier. A bellman carries luggage and does errands in a hotel.

The children also got jobs there during the summers when they came home from their school in Institute. One summer, Katherine was working as a personal maid to the hotel guests. One of the guests she helped was a French lady who often called friends in Paris, speaking to them in French. Katherine was studying the language in high school and understood what the lady was saying. When the French woman realized this, she walked the girl down to the resort kitchen. Katherine spent lunchtimes during work talking with the resort chef, who was also French from Paris. Those talks helped Katherine become even better at speaking French. When she returned to school, her language teacher was amazed at how well Katherine spoke French. She sounded like she was really from Paris.

Katherine loved math and liked studying in her high school. Some teachers there really guided her in ways that would help her later. A teacher named Miss Turner had taught geometry. Geometry is a branch of mathematics that deals with points, lines, angles, and shapes. Katherine was excited to take the course because Miss Turner encouraged and mentored many students in math. The time in Miss Turner's geometry class would prepare Katherine for more challenging work in college math classes.

Another faculty member who helped was the principal of the school. He promoted an interest in astronomy by pointing out constellations as they walked home from the campus. Constellations are special groups of stars that can be seen from the earth. Astronomy is the study of stars, planets, and other things in space. That knowledge would help Katherine when she became part of the programs to put men into space. Katherine studied hard and graduated from the high school in Institute at the age of 14. Now she was ready for college.

Counting on a Good Education

Katherine's performance in high school was so good that it earned her an academic scholarship at college. This paid for all her school bills and she enrolled at the West Virginia State. She was soon enjoying her studies and the people at the college. She joined a special group called a Greek sorority. The Black sorority's name came from Greek letters -Alpha Kappa Alpha. Katherine remained active in this group long after she finished college. However, she knew all the students and professors on the campus, not just those in Alpha Kappa Alpha. She liked being around the smart people there, she said. Trying to decide on a major - what she would mainly study - was next. She tried to decide between English, French, and mathematics. Then a mathematics professor at college told her in fun, "If you don't show up for my class, I will come and find you". She chose math as her major, but studied French also.

Another professor who took a special interest in Katherine was Dr. William W. Schiefflin Claytor. Claytor was a very smart man himself and had earned very high college degree. He had a Doctor of Philosophy (Ph.D) degree in mathematics, only the third black man to get to this advanced level. His research in special math areas and hard work impressed many people. However, other people rejected him because he was black and he had trouble finding jobs in the areas he wanted. He was offered at job and taught at West Virginia State College. He had to teach many courses and help the students in them. This did not leave much time or many resources for the further study of mathematics like he wanted. He was unhappy with that, but one thing that he liked during his three years at the college was his bright student, Katherine.

When she took his classes, he saw quickly how bright and curious she was. Katherine remembered, "Sometimes I could see that others in the class did not understand what he was teaching. So I would ask questions to help them. He'd tell me that I should know the answer, and I finally had to tell him that I did know the answer, but the other students did not. I could tell." He advised her about her math studies and made sure she took all the courses needed to get a good job. He even created special courses for her. He created one class in a type of geometry called analytic geometry just for her. She was the only student in the class because she was ready for advanced study! The course would help her when she worked in the space program at NASA. Claytor thought she would be a good research mathematician. A research mathematician wants to learn more about a particular area in math to add to the knowledge about it. Professor Claytor told her she would be good at this and that would help her be ready when a research job was offered.

At just eighteen years of age, in 1936, Katherine Coleman graduated from West Virginia State College. She earned a Bachelor of Science degree in both mathematics and

French. More than that, she graduated summa cum laude. That phrase is from a language called Latin and means "with highest honor". She had made the best grades and done the best work she could in college. She would return to college for a special reason later, but first, like her mother, she decided to be a teacher.

Counting the Costs

Katherine Coleman was prepared for a career in research math, but finding a job in the field was difficult. It was even harder for Katherine than for her mentor, Dr. Claytor. They had spoken on this during her classes with him. "But where will I find a job?" She had asked him. "That will be your problem," said her mentor.

Katherine faced two problems in finding a job in research math. One, she was black. Two, she was a women. Both things hurt her chances of being hired in the field.

At the time in the United States, African Americans did not have the rights they have now. Decades later, the Civil Rights Movement would help black people have more freedoms. But when Katherine graduated, they faced laws and prejudice that limited them. Segregation meant that black people were not supposed to do things in the same places as white people. They had to go to different schools, eat at different places, and stay at different hotels. They even had to drink at different water fountains and go to different bathrooms. Some places even made laws to keep them from voting! An idea called "separate but equal" meant places should be as good for African-Americans as other races. This was often did not happen with blacks getting run-down places

Katherine faced an addition prejudice being a woman. Businesses wanted to hire men, thinking that women should get married and be home with children. Some people thought that women could not work as well as men. When women did get a job, they were usually paid much less than men were. Married women had even less choice than single women; even some schools felt that women teachers should not be married. This affected Katherine too, because she had gotten married.

The Civil Rights Act of 1964 started changing this. It said, "All persons shall be entitled to the full and equal enjoyment of the goods, services, facilities ...of any place of public [services]... without [unfairness] or segregation... That meant businesses had to be fair to all whatever race, color, religion, or national origin they were. In another part of this act, it said the federal government could not be unfair because of what sex a person was either. The federal government is the folks who lead the whole country. This meant that all people were supposed to be treated right, including black people and women.

However, that law had not been passed when Katherine Coleman graduated and was looking for a job. Teaching in a school for blacks was one of the few jobs open to her. The only other jobs were being a maid, cook, or such in places like the Greenbrier Resort. So, she took a job teaching math - and playing piano - at a school in Marion, Virginia. Even a teaching job would have been denied her if the school knew she had gotten married.

Katherine Coleman had met James Goble, a Marion native, while he was on summer break from college. He was studying to become a teacher himself. The two fell in love and decided to get married... They did so without telling anyone, even her parents, so that Katherine would not lose her teaching job. Jimmy graduated from college too and became a chemistry teacher after that. Katherine later accepted an offer, for more pay, from a high school in Morgantown, West Virginia.

Katherine's time in college was not through yet, however. One day, Dr. John Davis, president of West Virginia State College, where Katherine had graduated, showed up at her classroom door. He had a very special opening for her.

Change was already coming in ending segregation. The West Virginia governor at the time, Homer Holt, decided to desegregate all-white West Virginia State, by choosing some special black students to attend this important state university. Dr. Davis was at the classroom to tell Katherine she was one of those special students, one of just three chosen. The other two were men working as school principals in other parts of West Virginia. She had been chosen because she was smart, appealing, and calm. So, that summer, Katherine enrolled in the university's math department. The two men enrolled in the law school. They saw each other as they signed up for courses, but did not meet after that. Katherine's mother moved in with her in Morgantown to encourage her daughter as she took on this new challenge.

Katherine's marriage was still a secret as she started graduate courses in 1940, but could not remain secret much longer. At the end of the summer session, she found out she and Jimmy were going to have their first child. While a marriage could remain a secret, her coming motherhood could not. So Katherine stopped her graduate school training, and then told her parents of her marriage and the coming baby. The couple soon welcomed the first of their three daughters: Joylette, Constance, and Katherine. For a time, Katherine stayed home and raised her family, happy with marriage and motherhood. In the summer of 1944, her husband Jimmy became ill from drinking untreated milk. He got well after some time, but was not able to return to teaching when school started. The school officials offered the contract to Katherine. Thus, she went back to teaching in 1944, but more changes were coming for Katherine. Both would bring big differences in her life.

Count Me In

In 1952, they were at the wedding of Jimmy's younger sister. At this event came the moment that would bring the biggest change for Katherine, Jimmy, and the girls. Eric Epps, Jimmy's brother in law, told them about jobs in Virginia, where the Epps family lived. He said he could get Jimmy a job at the shipyards. To Katherine, he mentioned a government facility nearby seeking black women math experts. The place was Langley Memorial Aeronautical Laboratory. This was where research was done by those working for NACA, the National Advisory Committee for Aeronautics.

NACA formed in 1915 to oversee all the research done in the United States on flight. The group quickly became a research facility in its own right. In 1935, females were first employed at Langley as computers. In those days, the term computer meant a person. They figured the math problems needed for the researchers. As the US entered World War II, about 500 people worked at Langley. The need for new workers became very important as the war continued. The number of employees quickly rose to 1500, three times as many as before. In 1943, the need for new workers was still rising, but the pool of white workers was dropping. President F. D. Roosevelt, spurred by black leaders, had earlier opened the defense industry to all people. So, this meant that the people at Langley hiring people could now hire African American workers. So, the call went out for black female skilled in math to work as computers. A space on the west side of Langley became the computing pool. The workers there became known as the West Computers. But being hired did not mean the black women were free from segregation. In preparing the building, signs marking certain bathrooms and areas of the cafeteria for "Colored" were ordered. "Colored" is one of the terms used for African Americans at that time. Still, the ladies were glad to have the work, especially since the salary was more than they would make at other jobs.

When World War II ended in 1945, around 3000 people worked at Langley. That number was reduced some as the war ended, but not too much and not for long. The government could see that airplanes were important to the defense of the country. In fact, the army unit known as the Army Air Corp in the war became a new branch of the military. The United States Air Force came into being in 1947. The women computers were important to the research being done to improve airplanes, their flight, and their abilities. It was not long before there were more job openings. More office space was needed and the West Computing group moved into a new building with two big spaces for them.

That was the situation as the Gobles thought about whether to move or not. Katherine and Jimmy were both teachers and felt it important to help black students learn and advance. Still, the salaries were not that high and it was hard to provide all the family needed. Katherine used her math skills to have money for their needs and extra for piano lessons and Girl Scouts. She could sew well and make clothes for herself and her girls. To earn more money, she and Jimmy were live-in help for a family that spent summers in the Virginia mountains. The extra cash helped the Goble family through the hardest months during the rest of the year. The move would mean Katherine and Jimmy would both have to leave the teaching jobs they loved. They would also have to move away from their families. Their daughters would no longer be near the grandparents who cared for them so much. However, Katherine's salary would be higher. Jimmy's job at the shipyard - a lot of ships for the United States Navy were built there - would be more stable. It would also pay more, which helped the family. There was one more thing that Katherine thought about as they decided what to do. The new job would be a chance for her to work as a research mathematician. It was the kind of job Dr. Claytor had talked of and prepared her for when she was at college. That chance excited the curiosity that was a special part of her personality. She told Jimmy, "Let's do it." He agreed and they got ready to move to Newsome Park, a black community near their new jobs. Jimmy became a painter in the shipyards and Katherine became a substitute math teacher while waiting for her research job to open up.

Katherine's application to work in the West Computing group had been approved in 1952, when the family moved. She was not given the job until the summer of 1953 though. The year between gave the family time to settle into their new area and new life. Katherine met many people from the area she taught in the high school. She met others when she became a part of the local chapter of her college sorority, Alpha Kappa Alpha. The family joined Carver Presbyterian church and got involved with a local community center. They gained a strong social support network from all these.

When Katherine started working at the computing area, she knew neighbors that worked there also. For three decades - that is 30 years - she rode to the job with a friend named Eunice Smith. They enjoyed the ride together and chatting about things. Katherine was glad to find that her new boss, Dorothy Vaughn, was also from West Virginia. In fact, Dorothy's family had rented a house right across from Katherine's parents. Their fathers had even worked together some as bellmen at the Greenbrier Resort. Dorothy was a good mathematician and had worked her way up from computer to being the boss of the unit. She became a good manager, another thing Katherine liked about her. Dorothy knew how to pick just the right person for a special assignment. She understood both their math skills and how well they worked with others.

For two weeks, Katherine learned about the computing job. She had sheets to fill in with data from equations set up by Dorothy or an engineer. An equation is a math statement with parts that are equal. An engineer is a person who uses science to solve problems useful in work or other life. Math is a large part of working on these problems and Katherine was very good at it. She was also calm and got along well with people, just the kind of person Dorothy was looking for. This soon helped Katherine get a new assignment at Langley.

Both Dorothy Vaughn and the engineers, who were white males, often visited the computing group, watching the ladies at work. When the Flight Research Division needed two new computers, Dorothy knew Katherine would be a good choice. She went immediately to the second floor where the Division was located. She had been happy to have the job at West Computing, but the new assignment was exciting. Important research was done there. Even if the transfer was just for a while, she knew she would like being with the experts. Some of the men Katherine worked with there had presented their work to top researchers in the field.

Looking for an empty desk while she waited for her new boss, Katherine was startled when the man nearby looked up and then left. She wondered if it was because she was black or because she was a woman. Maybe he had just finished his work, she thought, deciding not to dwell on it. Her father had taught her, "You are as good as anyone in this town, but you are no better than any of them." She remembered that lesson and chose instead to think about the good things that had happened to her. Katherine and the man soon found out they were both from West Virginia and became good friends.

The transfer was supposed to for just a short time, but six months later, Katherine was still working in the Flight Research Division. Dorothy Vaughn, the supervisor in West Computing, was actually still Katherine's boss. The job was on a six month trial and a successful finish to that period meant Katherine could be promoted. That would mean a raise in salary, so Dorothy needed to find out where Katherine would be assigned. Henry Pearson, a branch chief in Flight Research, needed to offer Katherine a permanent position or send her back. Henry was not a fan of women in the workplace, but the other engineers knew Katherine was good. They did not want to lose her. So, Henry offered her a position in his group, the Maneuver Loads Branch, a certain section in the Division. It was also known as the

Guidance and Control Branch. Katherine now officially worked there and got a salary increase too.

The Maneuver Loads Branch did research on the forces at work as an airplane moved out of or back into a stable, steady flight. They also worked to make the skies safer as more airplanes were used. Soon after she started work in the branch. Katherine helped the men figure out why a small plane crashed. She looked at a film record of the plane's flight, making notes of facts and figures. The engineers asked her to convert certain items to different measures. They also supplied her with equations to use on the data. She helped them in many ways, and at last they knew why the plane had crashed. It had flown across the path where a jet had traveled soon before. The air was still disturbed and made small plane trip and fall from the sky. The knowledge lead to changes in air traffic rules that helped make flying safer. Katherine read the final report with interest, glad to have been a part of the work. Always wanting to learn more, she asked the engineers lots of questions about what they did. They did not mind answering her, always glad to talk about the subject of flight. She read newspapers and magazines, like Aviation Week regularly. It helped her know how the work she was doing connected to what was happening with airplanes and flight. She did not just want to do the work she was told to, like some other women. She wanted to understand how it worked, why something worked - or why it did not. Her love of learning new things made her a valuable part of the team.

Always able to get along with people, Katherine really liked the people she worked with. She learned about them and what they did outside of work. They liked her too because they could see she was smart. Like Katherine, they liked smart people. However, Katherine still faced some barriers. When she wanted to go meetings so she could learn more, some men told her that women did not go to meetings. She asked them, "Is there a law?" She kept asking until the engineers finally let her come to the meetings.

Because Katherine had light skin and a West Virginia accent, people were sometimes not sure if she was black. But she was and had to make some decisions about the segregated areas that were still in place at Langley. She chose to ignore the "Colored" bathrooms. Some buildings did not have them anyway and the ones for whites were not marked. Katherine decided she could use those as well and did so even after the difference was pointed out. By bringing her lunch, she not only avoided the issue of the segregated cafeteria space, but saved money and ate healthier food. Katherine knew that some people and laws were unfair to African Americans. However, she did not let it stop her in her own life. She was confident in her math skills and confident about her life.

Don't Count on It

With Katherine's higher salary and Jimmy's stable painter's job, the family could think about moving to a house. They were living in Newsome Park, a type of apartments known as "the projects". They were called that because they were housing projects built by the government for lower income families. Now, many African American families wanted to own their own home. The Gobles decided to buy a section of land in an area of Hampton, Virginia and build a house. The couple and their daughters were very excited, but then Jimmy started getting sick again.

This illness was much worse than the one he had gotten from the bad milk. He had headaches that got worse, got very weak, and was not getting well. It took the doctors a long time to find out what was wrong with him. He had a tumor on his brain and it was located at a place where the doctors could not operate to remove it. He got more and more sick over the next year and spent a lot of time in the hospital. Just before Christmas in 1956, James Goble died. Jimmy and Katherine's parents, other family, and friends came to help the young widow and her three teenage daughters. They brought food, ran errands, and filled the church for Jimmy's funeral. However, they could not erase the grief the women felt at the early loss of their much loved husband and father. Katherine and her daughters were very sad whenever they remembered the event at Christmases after that.

Katherine was now a single mother and still wanted to raise her children like she and Jimmy had planned. So, she could not allow herself or the girls to give in to their sadness for too long. They could grieve fully just until the end of the year was Katherine's decision. When school started again in January, she met with the principal at her daughters' school. She told him, "It is very important that you don't show the girls any special treatment, or let up on them in any way. They are going to college, and they need to be prepared."

As a single mother now, Katherine was the only one earning money for the family. Joylette, Connie, and Kathy would have to help more around the house. Their mother made new rules saying, "You will have my clothes ironed and ready in the morning, and dinner ready when I come home." The girls not only helped at home, but continued with their music lessons, and made good grades in school. Katherine went back to her work, sad at the loss of her husband but ready to go on with her life and her job.

That job would become even more important on October 4, 1957. That was the date the Soviet Union put a satellite launched Sputnik I. It went into orbit around the earth, circling every nine-eight minutes. The Soviet Union, sometimes just called Russia, was a country many US citizens felt was dangerous. Americans were afraid that Sputnik would be used to find places for the Russians to drop bombs. Some built special protected underground shelters with food and supplies in case that happened. The Greenbrier Resort where Katherine and her father had worked had a very special place put underneath it. That place was to be used only by the government leaders of the US. That way they would be protected and still be able to run the country if something bad happened.

Leaders in the US government were upset that the Soviet Union sent up a satellite first. They felt the US was now playing catch-up in the "space race". The space race was the race between the US and the USSR to see who could get objects and men into space first. For the engineers and computers at NACA, it brought a big change. To this time, they had worked on making airplanes better and faster. For 40 years, they had helped develop everything from passenger jets to military fighter planes. They had even worked on planes that reached supersonic speeds. Supersonic means that the plane is going faster than the speed of sound through the air. It is traveling over 700 miles per hour mph). More of the testing of such planes was moving out west. The Dryden Flight Research Center in the Mojave Desert of California was a good place for this work. The workers at NACA had wondered what would happen to their jobs. Now they knew; they would start researching space travel.

Earlier, US leaders told the engineers not to waste time on space travel. They considered it science fiction. The researchers had thought about it anyway. They imagined how missile bodies might look and how rocket engines might work. They knew that first the rocket would have get through the earth's air to escape gravity. Gravity is the pull of the earth on things near its surface. Then the rocket would also face high friction when it was coming back into the earth's air -its atmosphere. Friction is when two things rub against each other; it usually makes those things get hot. Here, the capsule - the part of the rocket that would hold men - would rub against the air as it returned to earth. It would be going so fast that it would get really hot. So, the people studying space travel knew the rocket would have to be very powerful to lift off from the ground. It should also be made of very strong materials to protect it when it came back down.

One group at Langley suggested a reusable rocket, somewhat like the Space Shuttle that came later. Right now leaders wanted something that could get into space as quickly as possible. That way the US could start catching up with Russia. Another group, closely related to Katherine's Flight Research Division, was working on another type of rocket. This group was called the Pilotless Aircraft Research Division - PARD - and had even been testing things at a space near the coast. Their rockets had reached speeds of Mach 15 in flight. A Mach speed is figured from a math equation using the speed of an object and speed of sound. The supersonic planes that Katherine's group had helped with earlier went at a speed of Mach 1 or a bit more. Remember that those planes traveled a little over the speed of sound. That means the rockets being tested would going up to fifteen times more than the speed of sound. That is over 11,000 miles per hour! The engineers in PARD felt sure they could successfully launch a satellite and a human passenger into space.

People wanted action and wanted it soon; that meant, PARD and Flight Research now became very important again. Katherine shared an office with some of the men who would be very involved in engineering for the space program. They ate lunch together and talked of ideas and research for this assignment. Like them, Katherine wanted to get the United States back on top in getting into space. Even more than that, she liked being involved in this fresh area. It excited her interest because it was a brand new area to explore and learn about. Katherine's math skills would become even more important as the space program progressed.

There were other groups around the country working on rockets and space travel also. These included the US Air Force, the Army Ballistic Missile Agency, and the US Naval Observatory. An observatory is a place that studies stars and planets. The Army unit was run by a German man, Werhner Von Braun, whose work was crucial to the space program. When the government wanted a place to bring together the work from all the different groups, they chose Langley. In October 1958, the government brought all these groups, plus a group called the Jet Propulsion Laboratory, together. The new federal agency was named National Aeronautics and Space Administration. NACA officially became NASA. The Space Act of 1958 would rename the facility to Langley Research Center. An item stopping segregation there was included in the act. The next part of Katherine's amazing career began. Along with it a new chapter in her personal life started.

Count Down

Katherine and her daughters lived in the house built before James Goble died and were doing well. The girls were all talented musicians and honor students as well. Joylette had even graduated as salutatorian of her high school class. That means her grades were the second best in all that class. She was now headed to Hampton Institute to start college. Kathy and Connie were sophomores at the high school, preparing for college themselves. All four of them were polite and calm in others, but still sometimes lonely and sad. Katherine sometimes felt left out socially since she was a single mom while other neighbors were married couples. That was about to change though.

One night, Katherine was at choir practice at her church when a new singer came to join the group. The new person was a nice looking army captain named James Johnson. James had been born and raised in Virginia. He had even planned to attend Hampton Institute, the college Katherine's daughter Joylette was attending. During World War II, he had been drafted, or ordered, into the military. He went into the navy first and was trained to work with metal so he could repair airplane propellers. When his war service ended, he returned to school and got his college degree. He worked as a clerk in a US government office, but signed up for the Naval Reserves. Reservists are a special group of people who are available to help the regular military if needed. Jim wanted to do this so he could repair planes used in test flights. When the US entered a war in Korea, in Asia, Jim signed up to be part of the regular army. He worked on guns as an artillery sergeant. When that war ended, he came back to Hampton, near the Langley center where Katherine worked. He became a mail carrier for the US Post Office, but also signed up to be in the Army Reserves. Katherine and Jim had several things in common. They attended the same church and sang in the choir there. They also both had worked in jobs having to do with airplanes and aeronautics. They started dating and in 1959, they married. As a military man, Jim understood the extra demands of Katherine's job, such as long hours and secrecy. That was good because the first part of the new US space program was starting. It was called Project Mercury and Katherine's math expertise was needed more than ever.

The leaders of Project Mercury set three main goals for the program: to orbit a spacecraft with a person around the Earth, to learn about man's ability to function in space, and to recover both men and spacecraft safely. Seven special men were called up as the first astronauts. Four of them - Alan Shepard, John Glenn, Wally Shirra, Scott Carpenter - graduated from the US Naval Test Pilot School. This was where Jim Johnson had worked as a mechanic. The others were Virgil "Gus" Grissom, Gordon Cooper, and Donald "Deke" Slayton. The project ran from 1958 to 1963. During this time, six flights with a human were done. Others with no one aboard or with animal, like chimpanzees Ham and Enos, were also launched.

The different groups working on the space program had different tasks. The group under Von Braun used rockets from the army's inventory to prepare them to send a capsule with a man into space. Other groups worked on other systems and needs. Katherine's group worked with the people assigned trajectories. The trajectory is the path an object follows in traveling through space. Rockets needed to launch under specific conditions to follow a certain path in space. That was so the rocket would return to earth in a specific area where a ship would be waiting to pick it up. If the rocket came down in the wrong place, a ship might not get to it in time. The capsule - and more importantly its human crew- would be lost. A man who worked with Katherine transferred to a new unit working on Project Mercury. He soon found that the work load of the program was very heavy. So he sometimes asked his former co-workers help him. They liked working on space travel because it seemed like a lot of fun compared to what they usually worked on. They were to do computing runs, or math figuring, for him. That usually meant asking Katherine to do the math. She was reliable, experienced with computing trajectories, and could handle well the higher level thinking needed. She wanted to be a part of this new adventure just as much as the men did. One time she told them, "Tell me where you want the man to land, and I'll tell you where to send him up."

Another time, Katherine helped write a special report, a research report that would describe Project Mercury's orbital flight. It involved a lot of computing, descriptions, and figures. Katherine had to use not only her geometry math skills but the science of physics also. Physics is the study of matter and energy and the way they relate to each other. The man Katherine was working with on the report more and more worked with another group, so Katherine ended up doing a lot of the work on the report. When their boss asked about the unfinished item, the man told him, "Katherine should finish the report. She's done most of the work anyway." The work was read and studied and tested by many people before it became official. When it did, Katherine's name - her new married name of Katherine G. Johnson - was on the report. This was the first time in this division at Langley that a women's name went on such an important item. The report was important in helping NASA regain the lead over the USSR in the space race.

The space agency wanted to send a man into space, a suborbital - or less than a full circle around the earth - flight in 1961. The goal was made even more important by two events. The first happened when Russia again beat the United States into space. On April 12, 1961, cosmonaut (the Russian name for astronauts) Yuri Gagarin became both the first human in space and the first human to orbit Earth. The second happened the next month when new President John F. Kennedy set a special goal while talking to Senators and Representatives in the US Congress. He told them, "I believe that this nation should commit itself to achieving the goal, before this decade is out, of landing a man on the moon and returning him safely to the earth." That was a big dream since the US had not put a man into space at all yet.

The NASA employees had to continue to move forward, working hard if they were to put a man on the moon. The first step was putting an American into space. That man would be Alan Shepard, and Katherine would become a major worker in figuring out the trajectory of his flight. This flight involved a more basic flight plan based on a figure called a parabola. A parabola can look a bit like the letter u. In this case, the rocket trajectory looked like an upside down u or curve. To make sure the craft, with the person in it, came down at the right place, Katherine and the team needed to figure out when it should take off. This was called the launch window. Less than a month after Gagarin's flight, on May 5, 1961, Shepard strapped into the spacecraft that he had named Freedom 7. His light lasted just 15 minutes and 28 seconds, but it was important. His suborbital flight had successfully put the first American in space. NASA had bravely decided to show the launch on television and millions of people watched the history making flight.

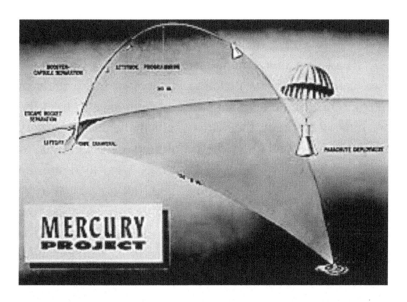

There were more flights to come and the next one, another suborbital flight, was in July, 1961. Virgil Grissom went up in a spacecraft known as Liberty Bell. That flight lasted 15 minutes and 37 seconds. Though the flight was successful, the craft sank shorting after splashing down in the ocean because of a problem with the hatch, or door. Grissom was safely rescued however. Liberty Bell 7 was finally raised out of the ocean in 1999, 38 years after it sank.

The next step was putting a man in orbit, a full circle around the earth. The man chosen for this important flight was John Glenn. The math Katherine would use for the path of this flight would be more complex. This was because more things would be affecting the craft, such as the gravity of other bodies in space and the rotation of the earth for a longer time. Katherine felt sure of her ability to do the job, but something new had been added at Langley. There were now machine computers as well as human computers.

These early machine computers were very large and people used cards with holes punched in them to make it run a calculation. Some astronauts did not completely trust the machines. They knew the human mathematicians, knew they did good work, and knew they could rely on them. One of those was Glenn. A machine had been used to figure the launch window and path for his flight, but he wanted to be sure those figures were right. "Get the girl to check the numbers," said the astronaut. If she says the numbers are good, I'm ready to go." Everyone knew he was talking about Katherine. She set to work checking all the math done by the other computer. It was all correct and the flight launch was set. On February 20, 1962, Glenn took off in a spacecraft he named Friendship 7. The flight lasted 4 hours, 55 minutes, and 23 seconds. He orbited the earth three times. The first American had gone into orbit. People considered Glenn a hero and he became well known, but Katherine's work was also praised. Stories about her were published in newspapers. African Americans were proud of the work done by her.

John Glenn

The Story of Katherine Johnson

Lady Mathematician Played Key Role in Glenn Space Flight

ONASA

There were three more flights in Project Mercury. Each one added to the knowledge of space travel. NASA was now ready for the next part of the program. This was called the Gemini program. It ran from 1962 to 1966, with nineteen craft launched. One change in the rockets was that the capsule could now hold two crew members instead just one. This program was used to test equipment and tasks and improve how the craft moved. It also tested the docking, or connecting, of two vehicles and the first American to do a spacewalk was one of the Gemini astronauts. A spacewalk is when a person goes outside of the spacecraft. All these missions were preparing for the next and final part of getting a man onto the moon - the Apollo program.

Mission Control

The Apollo program ran from 1967 to 1972 and launched eleven missions. The first four missions prepared for the one that would finally land on the moon. They tested the parts of the vehicle, now consisting of a command piece that would stay in orbit around the moon and the lunar piece that would actually go down to the surface of the moon. That part would then lift off and return so the two pieces could rejoin. Each spacecraft now held a crew of three.

Finally, the time came for the mission that would actually put a person on the moon. Apollo 11 launched in July of 1969 with astronauts Neil Young, Edwin "Buzz" Aldrin, and Michael Collins aboard. Armstrong and Aldrin were to go to the moon's surface while Collins would stay in orbit.

Katherine had done the math the flight, figuring the launch window and trajectory for the mission. She knew her numbers were right, yet she was nervous as well as excited following the news reporting of Apollo 11, knowing that things could still go wrong. On July 20, while at a special meeting with her sorority sisters, she watched as the two men walked on the moon. They were not just the first Americans, but the first men to do so at all. The United States had beaten the Russians at last and President Kennedy's goal had been reached! The two men spent over 21 hours on the moon, and then returned safely to the command portion for the flight back to earth.

There were six more missions in the Apollo program, with five of them reaching the moon.   Katherine not only continued to do computations for those flights but helped the one that did not make it to the moon still get back to earth safely. Apollo 13 was supposed to explore another part of the moon's surface, but an explosion on board the craft meant that the mission had to be stopped. The people at NASA were not even sure they could get the men back to earth. One problem was that the navigation system, the piece that directed their travel, was no longer working. However, earlier Katherine had helped figure out a way to find a path by using the stars that could be seen. Because of the wreckage from the explosion, the astronauts could not always be sure they were looking at stars, so the method could not be used. However, because she and others had thought about what could go wrong and what to do about it, one of the men had tried out another method on an earlier flight. He used this way and the crew got back to earth safely. The rest of the missions were all successful and Katherine had been an important part of that achievement.

Epilogue

Katherine Johnson stayed at NASA for fourteen more years, retiring in 1986. She stayed long enough to be a part of the next phase of space travel. That was the Space Shuttle program. Finally, the US worked on developing reusable craft that was suggested years before. The program lasted from 1981 to 2011, with five craft used.

Katherine regularly went to schools to talk about math and she how she used it in her career. She encouraged the students to study math and science and to do their best in school.

She received many awards and honors for her work. She earned many achievement awards from NASA. Colleges gave her honorary doctorate degrees. A STEM (science, technology, engineering, math) institute in North Carolina was named for her. A new research computing building at Langley was also named for her.

She received a special award in 2015. US President Barak Obama presented her with the Presidential Medal of Freedom. This is the highest honor a civilian (not in the military) can receive. It is for people who have made "especially meritorious contributions to the security or national interests of the United States, to world peace, or to cultural or other significant public or private endeavors."

Katherine remains polite and humble still, praising the achievements of others who worked at Langley rather than herself. She lives still with her husband Jim in their house in Hampton, Virginia. It is filled with pictures of her children and grandchildren.

President Barak Obama presented Katherine Johnson with the Presidential Medal of Freedom.

Despite her achievements and awards through an amazing career, she is still the "girl who loved to count".

Lessons from Katherine Johnson's Life

On Math:

Katherine not only liked math, she saw how important it was in her life. She used it at home as she worked on her family's budget during times when they were not making as much money. She made it stretch to meet both needs and some extras that were important like piano lessons. She used math at her job a lot as she worked with engineers. Her math skills were very important as she helped in the space program. The math even helped get men into space, to the moon, and back to earth.

On NASA and Science:

Katherine was proud to be part of the new space program when the National Aeronautics and Space Administration began. She thought people should keep learning and growing, even learning more about space by sending people there. She liked that she could use her math to help with the science of travel through air and space. She used the two subjects together to make sure astronauts landed where they were supposed to in order to be safe.

On Education:

Katherine always like learning. She went to the library and read a lot as a child. Reading helped her do well in school, even though she was also very smart. She stayed in school, graduating from college. She had taken lots of courses so she would know all about math. She was curious too, so she asked a lot of questions, as a child and an adult. At her job, she wanted to keep learning. So she asked the engineers about how things worked and why things worked like they did. She went to meetings with the men so she could better understand how math and science were used together in the research.

On Dealing with Prejudice:

Katherine faced people who did not think she was a good as they were. Some did not think black people should mix with white people. Katherine remembered the lesson her father taught her, that she was no worse and no better than anyone else. That gave her confidence and a right view of herself. Other people thought that women should not be working except as wives and mothers. Even some women were afraid to try to get better education or positions for themselves. Not Katherine though, she was not afraid to push, politely, to get ahead in life. She knew that women and African Americans were just as good as men and white people.

On Working Together:

Katherine believed in working with others as a team toward a goal. She and her husband were partners in raising their girls to be good students and good citizens. When she remarried, she and her new husband continued this process. Katherine also labored side by side with the engineers and other computers at NACA and NASA. She knew they were all working toward the same goal and believe everybody should do their best at their jobs. She thought people should help each other so the team could reach the goal.

On Living Your Dream:

Katherine had a dream about her life. She wanted to be educated, to have a family, to work at job with smart people. Most of all, she had the dream of a job like Dr. Claytor had prepared her for - research mathematician. She worked hard to make those dreams come true and be prepared when chances came her way. She liked having a challenge and believed in having a mission. Those came together in her job at NACA/NASA and she was ready for it. She liked her job and did her best at it.

Quotes from Katherine Johnson

On Math:

I counted everything. I counted the steps to the road, the steps up to church, the number of dishes and silverware I washed ... anything that could be counted, I did.

I knew they asked me to check the numbers. That was what I did. They knew my record for accuracy. I knew and had confidence in my math, so I did it. I always did my best.

We wrote our own textbook, because there was no other text about space. We just started from what we knew. We had to go back to geometry and figure all of this stuff out. Inasmuch as I was in at the beginning, I was one of those lucky people.

Everything is physics and math

On NASA and Science

I'm very proud of what they're doing and how they're doing it and why, [People ask] 'What good does it do us to go to space?' Well what good does it do you to stay home?

We were all dedicated to NASA, she said, and that came first.

Early on, when they said they wanted the capsule to come down at a certain place, they were trying to compute when it should start, Johnson said in an interview. I said, Let me do it. You tell me when you want it and where you want it to land, and I'll do it backwards and tell you when to take off. That was my forte.

Everybody was concerned about them getting [to the moon]. We were concerned about them getting back.

On Education:

[The male engineers] preferred the black mathematicians; they said we were better than the white girls. For one thing, all of us had been to college, whereas only some of the white women had.

I was always around people who were learning something. I liked to learn.

Just do it. Take all the courses in your curriculum. Do the research. Ask questions. Find someone doing what you are interested in! Be curious!

The fact that teachers can obstruct or they can assist. And mine always assisted me in moving up.

I finally persuaded [the librarians] to let me look at two books. I could have read more than that in one night if they had let me.

I teach you what the problem is, how to attack it — if you attack it properly you'll get the answer.

The women did what they were told to do. They didn't ask questions or take the task any further. I asked questions; I wanted to know why. They got used to me asking questions and being the only woman there.

I like to learn, she says. That's an art and a science. I'm always interested in learning something new.

On Dealing with Prejudice:

When the space program came along I just happened to be working with guys and then they had briefings on it, I asked permission to go. And they said 'well, the girls don't usually go.' I said 'well, is there a law?'

We learned to pick our battles for the greater good.

My dad taught us 'you are as good as anybody in this town, but you're no better.' I don't have a feeling of inferiority. Never had. I'm as good as anybody, but no better.

We needed to be assertive as women in those days - assertive and aggressive - and the degree to which we had to be that way depended on where you were. I had to be. In the early days of NASA women were not allowed to put their names on the reports - no woman in my division had had her name on a report. I was working with Ted Skopinski and he wanted to leave and go to Houston ... but Henry Pearson, our supervisor - he was not a fan of women - kept pushing him to finish the report we were working on. Finally, Ted told him, Katherine should finish the report, she's done most of the work anyway. So Ted left Pearson with no choice; I finished the report and my name went on it, and that was the first time a woman in our division had her name on something.

Girls are capable of doing everything men are capable of doing. Sometimes they have more imagination than men. Men don't pay attention to small things. They aren't interested in how you do it, just [in] give me the answer.

On Working Together:

I never took any credit because we always worked as a team, it was never just one person.

We did what we were asked to do to the best of our ability.

They needed information and I had it, and it didn't matter that I found it. At the time, it was just a question and an answer.

On Living Your Dream:

Luck is a combination of preparation and opportunity. If you're prepared and the opportunity comes up, it's your good fortune to have been in the right place at the right time and to have been prepared for the job.

Find out what her dream is and work at it because if you like what you're doing, you will do well.

I was just excited to have challenging work to do and smart people to work with.

You had a mission and you worked on it. And it was important to you to do your job.

Works Cited

"Katherine G. Johnson." *MAKERS*. AOL, n.d. Web. 28

Mar. 2017.

"Katherine Johnson: Visionary Videos: NVLP: African

American History." *Katherine Johnson: Visionary*

Videos: NVLP: African American History. National

Visionary Leadership Project, n.d. Web. 29 Mar.

2017.

Keating, Caitlin. "Hidden Figures' Real-Life NASA

Mathematician Katherine Johnson: 'If You Like

What You're Doing, You Will Do Well'."

PEOPLE.com. Time Inc, 29 Jan. 2017. Web. 29

Mar. 2017.

Loff, Sarah. "Katherine Johnson Biography." *NASA*.

NASA, 22 Nov. 2016. Web. 29 Mar. 2017.

Martin, Victoria St. "'Hidden' No More: Katherine Johnson,

a Black NASA Pioneer, Finds Acclaim at 98." *The*

Washington Post. WP Company, 27 Jan. 2017.
Web. 29 Mar. 2017.

"Meet the 'Hidden Figures' Mathematician Who Helped
Send Americans into Space." LA Times, n.d. Web.
29 Mar. 2017.

"NASA Missions A-Z." *Https://www.nasa.gov/missions*.
NASA, n.d. Web. 28 Mar. 2017.

Ott, Tim. "Katherine G. Johnson." *Biography.com*. A&E
Networks Television, 10 Oct. 2016. Web. 29 Mar.
2017.

"She Was a Computer When Computers Wore Skirts."
NASA, n.d. Web. 29 Mar. 2017.

Shetterly, Margot Lee. *Hidden Figures: The Untold Story
of the African American Women Who Helped Win
the Space Race*. London: William Morrow, an
Imprint of HarperCollins, 2017. Web.

Smith, Yvette. "Katherine Johnson: The Girl Who Loved to

    Count." *NASA*. NASA, 20 Nov. 2015. Web. 29 Mar.

    2017.

The Unbelievable Life of the Forgotten Genius Who Turned

    Americans' Space Dreams into Reality. Business

    Insider, n.d. Web. 29 Mar. 2017.

Wild, Flint. "Katherine Johnson: A Lifetime of STEM."

    NASA. NASA, 16 Nov. 2015. Web. 29 Mar. 2017.

Dear Reader,

If you enjoyed this book or found it useful, I would be very grateful if you would post a short review on Amazon. Your support really does make a difference and I read all the reviews personally so I can get your feedback and make this book even better.

If you would like to leave a review, all you need to do is click the review link on this book's Amazon page here.

If you are a member of kindleunlimited, I would be most grateful if you would scroll to the back of the book so I will be paid for your borrowed book.

Thanks again for your support.

America Selby

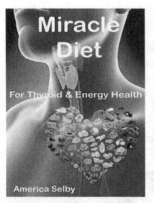

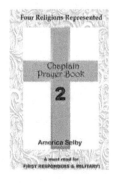

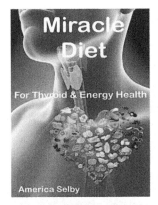

Miracle Diet

For Thyroid & Energy Health

America Selby

HAPPY BIRTHDAY III
Adult & Children's Coloring Book

Happy Birthday

day
month
year

America Selby

Inspirational

Adult Coloring Book Series Book II

FREEDOM

America Selby

HOW TO GET GOOD GRADES
IN HIGH SCHOOL

& OTHER PARENT'S QUESTIONS

D. RICE

Keeping Ducks

The Secret to Successfully
Raising & Keeping Ducks

America Selby

VINTAGE HOLIDAY
ADULT COLORING BOOK

AMERICA SELBY

Made in the USA
Columbia, SC
16 April 2020